STRANGE AND AMAZING INSECTS

LEVEL  READER

READING LEVEL
2
GRADES 1 TO 3

Written by Kathryn Knight

Franklin, Tennessee 37068-2068. 1-866-418-2572.
No part of this book may be reproduced or copied in any form without written permission
from the copyright owner. CE12988/1011

Hissssss!

Insects are amazing. Some change from one form to another. Some can survive extreme cold or heat. Some have been around for millions of years. And some are just plain strange!

On the island of Madagascar there are huge 3-inch roaches. If you hold one (they're harmless) and slightly squeeze it, it will hiss—loudly!

Gromphadorhina portentosa, hissing cockroach of Madagascar, Africa

Giraffe Weevil

Weevils are long-snouted little insects. But there's one in Madagascar that is long-necked. The male giraffe weevil is one of the strangest-looking bugs around. It goes through life quietly, calmly munching leaves. It is not one to "stick its neck out," and this one-inch critter will scuttle away if it senses danger.

Trachelophorus giraffa, weevil of Madagascar, Africa

Dragonfly

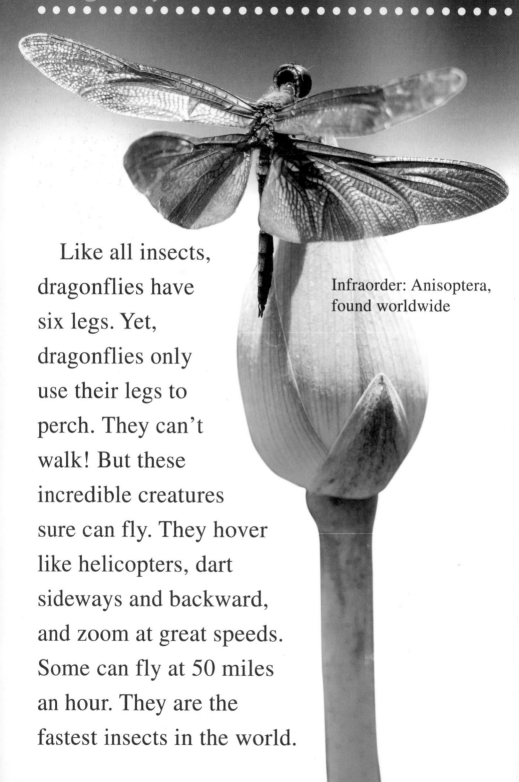

Like all insects, dragonflies have six legs. Yet, dragonflies only use their legs to perch. They can't walk! But these incredible creatures sure can fly. They hover like helicopters, dart sideways and backward, and zoom at great speeds. Some can fly at 50 miles an hour. They are the fastest insects in the world.

Infraorder: Anisoptera, found worldwide

Fireflies are a common sight at night in spring and summer. And these little blinkers are amazing! They make their own light inside their bodies. This is a "cold light." It gives off no heat at all. The light says, "Here I am, other fireflies!"

Family: Lampyridae, found worldwide

In June in the Great Smoky Mountains, you can watch as fireflies blink on and off— all at the exact same time.

Next time you pick up a leaf in Australia or Asia, check to see if it has legs. There are walking leaves out there! Birds and reptiles walk right past these tasty meals, thinking they are part of the plant.

The trick of blending in with plants, dirt, or rocks is called *camouflage* (**kam**-oh-flahj). Leaf insects are the best in the world at camouflage!

Family: Phylliidae, of Asia and Australia

Spiny Leaf Insect

This odd creature is actually a "stick" insect, but it looks like dried leaves. The female has spikes that camouflage her among thorny plants. Like leaf insects, these fellows will slightly sway back and forth, like leaves moving in the breeze. Clever little critters!

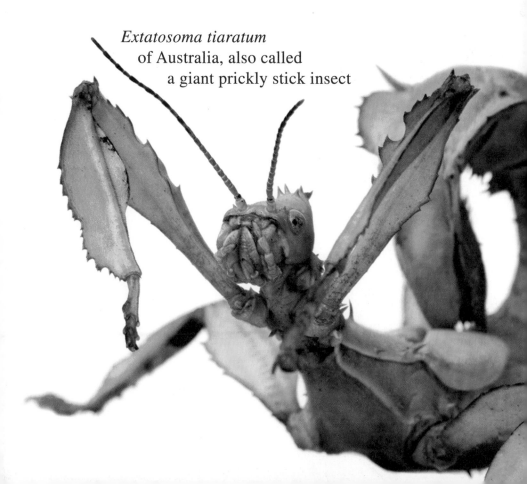

Extatosoma tiaratum of Australia, also called a giant prickly stick insect

A nymph (nimff) is a graceful, shy, fairy-like girl of the woods. But not this nymph! This creature is big, bulky, and bossy. It is 6 inches long with thorny spikes on its thick body. The female will hiss and attack if you bother her.

Heteropteryx dilatata of Australia and Malaysia

Walking Stick

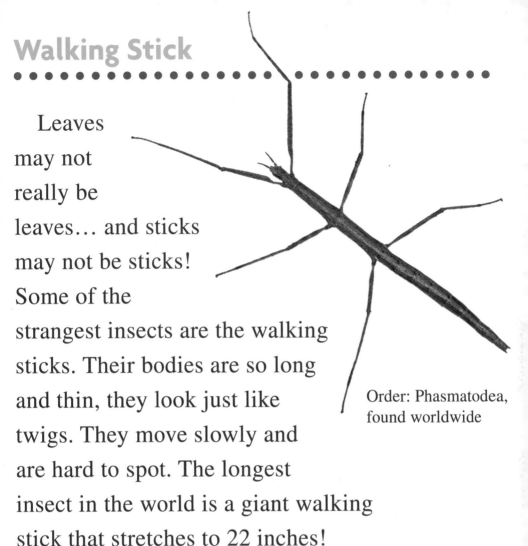

Leaves may not really be leaves… and sticks may not be sticks! Some of the strangest insects are the walking sticks. Their bodies are so long and thin, they look just like twigs. They move slowly and are hard to spot. The longest insect in the world is a giant walking stick that stretches to 22 inches!

Order: Phasmatodea, found worldwide

Titan Beetle

• •

The world's longest beetle is the titan. This longhorn beetle of South America can be 6½ inches long. It is fast and powerful! Its strong *mandibles* (jaws) can cut a finger to the bone— or even snap a pencil in two! Yet, these giants don't eat in their adult beetle stage. They fly around to find a mate and then lay eggs.

Titanus giganteus of South America

Goliath Beetle

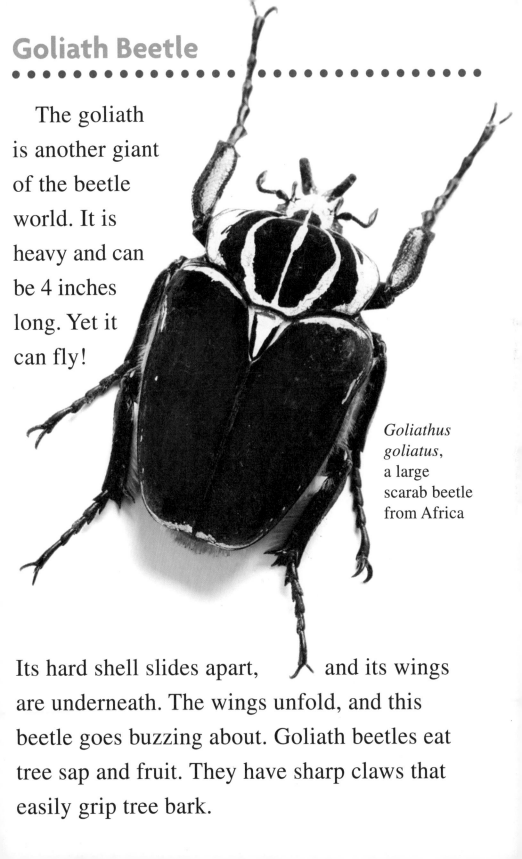

The goliath is another giant of the beetle world. It is heavy and can be 4 inches long. Yet it can fly!

Goliathus goliatus, a large scarab beetle from Africa

Its hard shell slides apart, and its wings are underneath. The wings unfold, and this beetle goes buzzing about. Goliath beetles eat tree sap and fruit. They have sharp claws that easily grip tree bark.

Elephant Beetle

There are more beetles in the world than any other kind of insect. And some are strange and amazing! The long horn of this big male looks like an elephant's trunk. The elephant beetle uses its horn to battle other males for females and food. Its shell is actually black. A coat of tiny golden hairs makes it look brown.

Megasoma elephas of Texas, Central and South America, and Australia

Rhinoceros Beetle

The elephant beetle is in the same family as all the rhinoceros beetles. Male rhino beetles have one or two horns, and they are very strong insects. Rhino beetles live for about a year and are sometimes kept as pets. They look fierce, but they are harmless to people. Feed them bananas and pineapple and they'll be happy bugs.

Oryctes nasicornis, the European rhinoceros beetle

Hercules Beetle

The largest rhinoceros beetle is the Hercules (**Her**-cue-leez) beetle. From its rump to the end of its horns, a male Hercules beetle can be more than 6 inches long. This "strongman" can lift objects that are 850 times its own weight. That would be like a 100-pound child lifting 17 African elephants!

Dynastes hercules of Central and South America

Stag Beetle

The male stag beetle has antlers! Well, not really. Those long, curved "horns" are part of its jaw. Stag beetles use these to wrestle with other males. Sometimes they compete for a female, sometimes for food. Stag beetles can be 2 to 4 inches long.

Lucanus elaphus
of North America

Treehopper

There are more than 3,200 kinds of treehoppers, and they all have their own look. These little fellows suck juices from plants, and they hide well on the plants they live on. Treehoppers are *mimics* (copycats). Some look exactly like thorns, little leaves, or parts of twigs. There is one kind that looks like an ant!

Family: Membracidae, found in the tropics worldwide

Spittlebug and Froghopper

Have you ever seen a glob of bubbles on a plant? That's a spittlebug nest. Spittlebugs suck plant sap and turn it into foam to hide in. Spittlebugs then change into froghoppers, the champion jumpers of the insect world. Froghoppers spring from leaf to leaf. Some leap 25 inches straight up. That's like a 7-year-old leaping over a 40-story building!

Superfamily: Cercopoidea, found in woodlands and grasslands worldwide

Mantis

It's fun to spot a praying mantis on a leaf or windowsill. These insects are odd-looking, yet handsome, don't you think? A mantis will watch you carefully, tilting its triangle-shaped head. It may hold its arms up as if it's praying. But it's really "preying." It can grab a bug in the blink of an eye and chew it up.

Order: Mantodea,
found worldwide

Hymenopus coronatus,
orchid mantis of
Southeast Asia

Mantises look a little like walking sticks and grasshoppers. But they are really more related to roaches and termites. Mantises eat insects. Some large 4-inch mantises will prey on small lizards, frogs, birds, and fish!

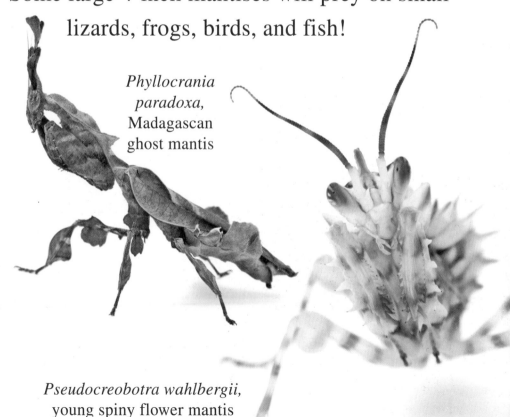

*Phyllocrania
paradoxa,*
Madagascan
ghost mantis

Pseudocreobotra wahlbergii,
young spiny flower mantis
of Africa

Cicada

Family: Cicadidae,
found worldwide

Cicada (sih-**kay**-duh) means buzzer. In the summer, male cicadas "sing" and fill the air with a loud ZZZZZ for hours and hours.

The most amazing thing about some cicadas is their age. After they hatch, they tunnel into the ground and live there for 13 or 17 years! Then they tunnel back up, become adult cicadas, and start singing!

Termite Queen

Cicadas may live for 17 years, but this lovely lady can live 50 years—or more! She is a termite queen. She looks like a big blob. She is so filled with eggs, she can't walk. Her workers clean and feed her. She may lay millions of eggs in her long lifetime.

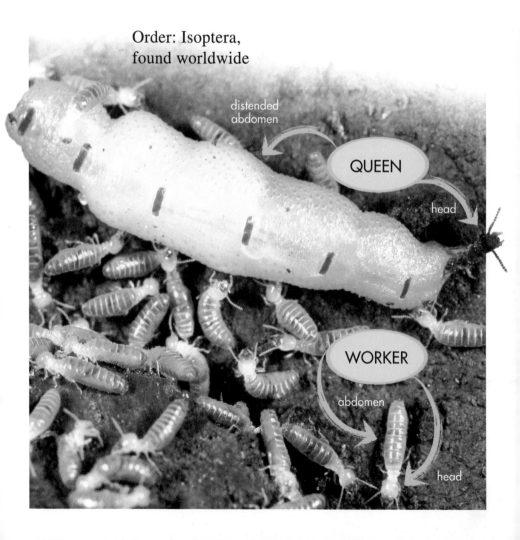

Order: Isoptera, found worldwide

distended abdomen

QUEEN

head

WORKER

abdomen

head

Army Ant

Most ants build a nest in the ground where the queen and all the young live. But not army ants. Army ants stay on the move. They march in a long path. Any creature in their way does not stand a chance. Army ants will attack and eat it!

When army ants come to a puddle or an object to climb, they link and form ant ladders. All the other ants walk across them!

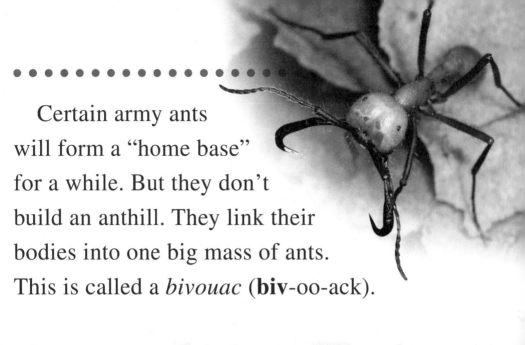

Certain army ants will form a "home base" for a while. But they don't build an anthill. They link their bodies into one big mass of ants. This is called a *bivouac* (**biv**-oo-ack).

Eciton burchellii and other species, found in the tropics worldwide

Honey Bee

Perhaps the most amazing insect is the honey bee. It's the only insect that makes a food people eat. Honey bees take pollen from flower to flower, helping plants and fruits to grow. And honey bees "talk" to each other. When a bee finds some good flowers, it waggle-dances in the hive. This dance tells the others where to go. Dance on, honey bees!